TRACEY GRUMBACH

He Shall Be Called

A 25-Day Advent Devotional for Praying the Names of Jesus

VERITAS
IGNITE REVIVAL
SPRING

For my Savior,
who is all these Names and more —
the One who found me, healed me, and called me His own.
And for my husband, Brian,
whose courage and faith have shown me what it truly means to
trust the Great Healer.
You are living proof that grace is stronger than fear.
May every page of this devotional point hearts to the One who came,
who still comes,
and who will come again.

"At the name of Jesus every knee should bow, in heaven and on earth and under the earth."

— Philippians 2:10 (NIV)

Contents

Preface

This devotional was born in a season of waiting.

It wasn't the kind of waiting marked by candlelight and carols, but the kind that presses against the heart — the waiting that comes with illness, uncertainty, and nights spent praying for miracles. During those quiet, aching months, I found myself clinging to the names of Jesus like lifelines. Each one reminded me that God's character never changes, even when my circumstances do.

I began writing *He Shall Be Called: A 25-Day Advent Devotional for Praying the Names of Jesus* not as an author trying to fill pages, but as a believer seeking peace in my own life and circumstances. I needed to remember that Jesus is not only the Wonderful Counselor who listens, but the Mighty God who sustains. That He is both the Healer and the Hope-giver, both the Lamb who suffered and the Lion who reigns.

The deeper I went, the more I realized that Advent is not just a countdown to Christmas — it's a journey of rediscovering who He is. Every name of Jesus tells a story. Together, they weave the extraordinary story of redemption, the one that began before time and continues in us today. My prayer is that this book will draw you close to the heart of Christ in both joy and hardship. Whether you're lighting candles, baking cookies, or simply trying to catch your breath in a busy season, may these daily reflections remind you that He is near.

He came once as a child. He comes now as a Friend, a Father, a Guide, and a Master. And one day, He will come again as King of Kings. May these pages lead you to worship the One who holds every name — and every heart — in His hands.

Introduction

Introduction — The Promise in a Name

Names carry power. They hold memories, meanings, and entire stories within a single word. In Scripture, they're never random. Each name God gives reveals something about who He is — His nature, His purpose, His heart for His people. Long before a star hung over Bethlehem, the prophets spoke of the coming Messiah through His names. *Wonderful Counselor. Mighty God. Prince of Peace.* Every title was a promise. Each one offered a glimpse of redemption before the Redeemer arrived.

Then, on a silent night in an ordinary town, every prophecy breathed its first cry. The Word became flesh. The One who had been whispered about for generations was finally here. *He Shall Be Called: A 25-Day Advent Devotional for Praying the Names of Jesus* invites you to walk slowly through twenty-five names of Jesus — one for each day of Advent. Each name reveals another facet of His character: the Shepherd who guides, the Light who conquers darkness, the King who reigns in love. Together, they form a portrait of the God who came near. Although you can go through each day's devotional in about 10 minutes, it is most potent when you take the time to digest all that's offered. It's a devotional that invites you to pause, take a breath, and return to wonder. Read each day with your morning coffee or before the quiet settles at night. Linger over the Scriptures. Let His names speak personally to your story.

As you move through these pages, you'll discover something remarkable: every name of Jesus tells us not just who *He* is, but who we are in Him. The Prince of Peace brings peace to our restless hearts. The Bread of Life nourishes our hunger for meaning. The Resurrection and the Life promises that even our darkest valleys can bloom again. So take your time. Let the season slow you down. Speak His names aloud — they are promises, power, and invitation all at once.

Because when you know His names, you begin to understand His heart. And that changes everything.

December 1

Wonderful Counselor

Scripture Focus:

> *"For to us a child is born, to us a son is given, and the government will be on his shoulders.*
> *And he will be called Wonderful Counselor, Mighty God, Everlasting Father, Prince of Peace."*
> *— Isaiah 9:6 (NIV)*

Reflection

Advent begins in the quiet — not with fanfare, but with longing. The people of Israel waited under the weight of silence, centuries deep. No prophets spoke. No miracles stirred—just the ache of anticipation and the whispered hope that God would remember His promise.

Then, through Isaiah, heaven broke its silence: *"He shall be called Wonderful Counselor."*

It's a breathtaking name. In Hebrew, *pele yo'etz* paints a portrait far beyond pleasant advice. *Pele* means "miraculous," "beyond comprehension," the kind of wonder that stops you mid-sentence. *Yo'etz* means "counselor," one who gives wisdom and guidance. Together, they reveal a Savior whose wisdom is both divine and deeply personal — the kind that knows your heart even when you can't find the words.

The Wonderful Counselor doesn't offer generic comfort from afar. He entered our world of sin and confusion, clothed Himself in flesh, and lived among us. He understands the human mind because He shaped it. He understands sorrow because He carried it. He understands your heart because He wrote its rhythm.

When life unravels and the noise of uncertainty grows loud, Christ doesn't merely hand out directions. He *is* the direction. He doesn't just provide clarity. He *is* the clarity. Every piece of wisdom we need for our next step rests not in our own understanding but in His character. Look at the Gospels and see His counsel in action.

- To the woman caught in sin, He said, *"Neither do I condemn you; go and sin no more."*
- To the fearful storm, He said, *"Peace, be still."*
- To His weary disciples, *"Come to Me, all who are burdened, and I will give you rest."*

That is the voice of the Wonderful Counselor — steady, compassionate, and sure.

He doesn't speak from a distance but from within our circumstances, guiding us not around pain but *through* it. Maybe this Advent meets you in the middle of something you don't understand — a loss you didn't expect, a prayer still unanswered, or a crossroad that feels unclear. Friend, you don't need to figure it all out. You only need to lean in and listen to the One who knows your heart.

The Wonderful Counselor doesn't ask you to perform, prove, or plan. He invites you to trust. To be still. To bring your confusion into His light and let His wisdom unfold in His time.

As you journey through these twenty-five days, remember: Advent isn't just about waiting for Christmas morning. It's about learning to wait *with* the One who already holds the outcome. And that Counselor — that Miracle of Wisdom — walks beside you even now.

Daily Affirmation-

Jesus is my Wonderful Counselor — infinitely wise, deeply compassionate, and perfectly patient with my heart.

Prayer

Lord Jesus, my Wonderful Counselor, thank You for being the wisdom my soul longs for. When I am overwhelmed by questions, remind me that You hold every answer. Quiet my anxious thoughts and tune my ears to hear Your voice above the noise. Teach me to trust the guidance of Your Spirit even when I can't see where it leads. You are not just the Giver of wisdom — You are Wisdom itself. Lead me, Lord, and I will follow. Amen.

Journaling Prompt

- What situation in your life right now needs divine wisdom more than human understanding?
- What might it look like to *listen* for God's counsel this week rather than rush for quick solutions?
- Write a short prayer of surrender, asking Jesus to take the lead in one specific area of uncertainty.

Verse to Write

> *"Trust in the Lord with all your heart and lean not on your own understanding;*
> *in all your ways submit to him, and he will make your paths straight."*
> — *Proverbs 3:5–6 (NIV)*

Reflection Break

Light a candle today as a symbol of His wisdom breaking through your darkness. Whisper His name — "Wonderful Counselor." Let His peace settle in the space between your questions and His answers.

December 2

Mighty God

Scripture Focus:

> *"For to us a child is born, to us a son is given, and the government will be on his shoulders.*
> *And he will be called Wonderful Counselor, Mighty God, Everlasting Father, Prince of Peace."*
> *— Isaiah 9:6 (NIV)*

Reflection

The same prophecy that named Jesus our Wonderful Counselor also calls Him *El Gibbor* — *Mighty God.* Those two Hebrew words are a thunderclap of power and divinity. *El* is the common Old Testament word for "God," and *Gibbor* means "strong one," "warrior," or "hero." Isaiah's original audience would have heard this as a declaration that the promised Messiah was not just empowered *by* God — He *was* God.

That truth alone was revolutionary.

No prophet, priest, or king in Israel's history ever bore a name like that. David was mighty in battle, but he was mortal. Moses spoke face-to-face with God, but he was still dust. The coming Messiah, Isaiah declared, would be divine in nature and infinite in power — a warrior who would conquer not by sword, but by salvation.

Centuries later, the angel Gabriel told a young woman in Nazareth that she would bear a son who would reign forever. That baby who was fragile, helpless, wrapped in cloth, was the Mighty God Himself. The One who spoke galaxies into being now cried in a manger. The same hands that carved out mountains reached for His mother's embrace.

What kind of God trades a throne for straw? What type of warrior enters the battlefield of sin and death as a newborn? Only a God whose might is measured not by force, but by love.

Throughout His ministry, Jesus revealed what divine strength looks like. He calmed seas with a word, healed diseases with a touch, and cast out demons with authority that made hell tremble. Yet His most remarkable display of might came on a cross where He willingly bore the full weight of sin to break its grip on humanity. The nails didn't prove weakness; they proved resolve. The tomb didn't signal defeat; it marked the beginning of victory.

The Mighty God fights battles the world cannot see — for hearts, for souls, for eternity. He is not merely powerful *out there*; He is powerful *in here*, in your story, your struggle, your sanctification.

When your strength falters, He stands. When your faith feels small, His power fills the gap. The same Mighty God who shattered death's hold now dwells within you by His Spirit. He doesn't just fight for you, He fights *through* you.

Advent reminds us that the baby born in Bethlehem is not just tender and kind; He is fierce in His mercy, unstoppable in His purpose, and victorious in His love.

This child is no ordinary king. He is the Mighty God — warrior, Savior, and Lord of all.

Daily Affirmation

Jesus is my Mighty God. He is victorious over sin, sovereign over all creation, and strong when I am weak.

Prayer

Mighty God, thank You for revealing strength through humility and power through love. When I feel weary or overwhelmed, remind me that You have already conquered the battles I fear. Teach me to rely on Your power, not my own. Be my defender, my refuge, and my source of courage. You are the strength of my heart and the hope of my salvation. Amen.

Journaling Prompt

- Where have you seen God's strength in your life — either through protection, provision, or endurance?
- What battle do you need to surrender to your Mighty God today?
- Write a declaration of faith, naming one area where you will trust His power over your own.

Verse to Write

> *"The Lord is my strength and my song; he has given me victory.*
>
> *This is my God, and I will praise him—my father's God, and I will exalt him."*
> — *Exodus 15:2 (NLT)*

Reflection Break

Light your second candle and whisper His name — "Mighty God." Picture the manger and remember that the One who came so gently is also the One who reigns in unshakable power. Rest in His strength today.

December 3

Everlasting Father

Scripture Focus:

> *"For to us a child is born, to us a son is given, and the government will be on his shoulders.*
> *And he will be called Wonderful Counselor, Mighty God, Everlasting Father, Prince of Peace."*
> *— Isaiah 9:6 (NIV)*

Reflection

There is something tender and intimate about the title *Everlasting Father.*

At first glance, it can be confusing — after all, Isaiah is describing the coming *Son.* How could the Messiah, the Son of God, also be called *Father*? But Isaiah isn't blurring the lines between the persons of the Trinity; he's describing the **character** of the coming King.

In Hebrew, the phrase is *Avi-'ad* — literally, "Father of Eternity." It means the One who authors and sustains all time, the Creator who holds eternity in His hands. When Isaiah called the Messiah "Everlasting Father," he wasn't confusing Jesus with God the Father, but that He carries the *heart* of a father — protective, faithful, and unending in His care for His children.

Jesus embodied that nature perfectly.

He gathered the broken. He wept with the grieving. He defended the vulnerable. He taught His followers to pray to *"Our Father in heaven,"* revealing the tender nature of God's relationship with His people.

Throughout His ministry, His actions reflected fatherly love, the kind that sees, protects, and provides. Consider His words in John 10:28: *"I give them eternal life, and they shall never perish; no one will snatch them out of my hand."* That is the voice of a Father's heart: strong, steady, protective. He guards what belongs to Him.

The world offers many temporary fathers: mentors, leaders, authorities — but none that last. People fail. Time fades. Yet Jesus, our Everlasting Father, remains constant. He doesn't abandon His own. His love doesn't diminish over the years or weaken under the weight of our failures. It is eternal because He is eternal.

When life feels unstable, remember that your Everlasting Father is not a reflection of your earthly experiences; He is the perfection of what fatherhood was meant to be. He is present when others leave, patient when you falter, and faithful even when you forget. From the cradle to the cross to the crown, Jesus has always been the author of eternity and the Father who holds time itself together. And somehow, in His infinite love, He has chosen to hold *you,* too. This Advent, rest in the arms of your Everlasting Father — the One who has never stopped seeing you, loving you, or calling you His own.

Daily Affirmation

Jesus is my Everlasting Father — constant in love, unchanging in His care, and eternal in His promises.

Prayer

Everlasting Father, thank You for loving me with a love that has no beginning and no end. You see every moment of my life, yet You never turn away. Heal the places in my heart that have been wounded by imperfect love, and teach me to rest in the security of Yours. Remind me that I am never alone, never forgotten, and always held in Your eternal care. Amen.

Journaling Prompt

- How does knowing Jesus as your Everlasting Father change your view of God's character?
- Have you ever struggled to trust God's love because of past experiences with earthly fathers or authority figures?
- Write a letter of gratitude to your Everlasting Father, thanking Him for the ways He has guided, protected, or comforted you.

Verse to Write

> *"As a father has compassion on his children, so the Lord has compassion on those who fear him."*
> — *Psalm 103:13 (NIV)*

Reflection Break

Light your third candle and whisper His name, "Everlasting Father." Picture His steady hands holding your past, present, and future all at once. Rest in the truth that His love for you will never run out.

December 4

Prince of Peace

Scripture Focus

For to us a child is born, to us a son is given, and the government will be on his shoulders.

And he will be called Wonderful Counselor, Mighty God, Everlasting Father, Prince of Peace.

— Isaiah 9:6 (NIV)

Reflection

Peace. It's a word that sounds soft on the surface, yet its biblical meaning runs deep and strong. The Hebrew word Isaiah used is *shalom* — a word far richer than simple calm or the absence of conflict. *Shalom* means wholeness, completeness, harmony, and restoration. It describes the way things are when everything is as God intended them to be.

When Isaiah prophesied that the coming Messiah would be

called the *Prince of Peace*, his audience was living in anything but peace. War, corruption, and fear defined their days. Yet God was not promising a temporary truce, but a King who would bring lasting reconciliation between God and humanity, and one day, throughout all creation.

Centuries later, when angels appeared to shepherds on a Bethlehem hillside, they declared, "Glory to God in the highest heaven, and on earth peace to those on whom his favor rests" (Luke 2:14). This was the fulfillment of Isaiah's prophecy. The Prince of Peace had arrived — not in royal splendor, but in humility. The One who spoke galaxies into being came quietly, wrapped in cloth, to still the war between heaven and earth.

Jesus didn't bring peace by avoiding conflict; He brought peace by conquering it. On the cross, He absorbed the wrath of sin, reconciling us to the Father. The peace He gives isn't a fleeting feeling; it's a new relationship with God. It is the restoration of what was broken since Eden. As Paul wrote, "He himself is our peace" (Ephesians 2:14).

This peace also transforms the heart. In a world that glorifies chaos and anxiety, Christ offers stillness that circumstances can't touch. His peace is not the calm after the storm; it's the calm *within* the storm. It anchors the soul when everything else shakes.

Maybe this Advent finds you in a season of unrest — tensions in your home, worry about the future, or the ache of loss. The Prince of Peace doesn't promise a life without struggle, but He does promise His presence within it. Peace is not found in perfect conditions; it is found in perfect trust. The same Jesus who calmed the raging sea speaks peace over the turbulence of your heart today. His rule is gentle, His reign unending, and His peace eternal. He is not only the giver of peace, He is Peace itself.

Daily Affirmation

Jesus is my Prince of Peace — my heart's calm in the storm, my steady assurance in uncertainty, and my reconciliation with God.

Prayer

Prince of Peace, thank You for entering this broken world and restoring what sin destroyed. Teach me to rest in Your presence when life feels unsettled. Quiet the noise within me, and let Your peace rule in my heart and home. Help me reflect Your peace to others this season, so that through me, they may see the power of Your gentle reign. Amen.

Journaling Prompt

- What circumstances in your life steal your sense of peace most easily?
- How can you remind yourself daily that Jesus Himself is your peace, not your situation?
- Write a short prayer inviting the Prince of Peace to reign over one area of conflict or anxiety in your life today.

Verse to Write

> *Peace I leave with you; my peace I give you. I do not give to you as the world gives.*
> *Do not let your hearts be troubled and do not be afraid.*
> *— John 14:27 (NIV)*

Reflection Break

Light your fourth candle and speak His name aloud — Prince of Peace. Sit in silence for a moment and let His stillness settle over you. The same peace that ruled the manger and the cross rules your heart today.

December 5

Emmanuel (God With Us)

Scripture Focus

"The virgin will conceive and give birth to a son, and they will call him Emmanuel" (which means "God with us").
— Matthew 1:23 (NIV)

Reflection

The name *Emmanuel* first appeared in a dark chapter of Israel's history. King Ahaz of Judah faced invasion and feared destruction. In that moment of national panic, the prophet Isaiah declared that a sign would come: a virgin would bear a son, and His name would be *Emmanuel*—God with us (Isaiah 7:14). For Ahaz, it was a promise of deliverance; for the world, it became a prophecy of hope.

Centuries later, those words came alive in Bethlehem. The Creator stepped into His creation. The infinite became an infant.

The One who once spoke the universe into being now cried within it. Through the birth of Jesus, God made His dwelling among us not as an idea, but as a person who could be seen, touched, and known.

Throughout Scripture, the presence of God marked every turning point of redemption. In the garden, He walked with Adam and Eve. In the wilderness, His presence appeared as a pillar of cloud and fire. In the temple, His glory rested between the cherubim. But in Jesus, that presence took on human form and moved into our neighborhood. He was no longer above us or beyond us. He was *with* us—shouldering our burdens, feeling our sorrows, and sharing our humanity.

To the lonely, Emmanuel means you are not forgotten. To the fearful, it means you are not abandoned. To the sinner, it means you are not beyond reach. The God who once dwelt in unapproachable light now meets you in the ordinary spaces of your life: in the quiet kitchen morning, the hospital waiting room, the long drive home.

Jesus' presence changes everything. He did not come to remove hardship, but to walk beside us through it. His nearness gives courage, His Spirit brings comfort, and His promise assures us that no matter how uncertain tomorrow feels, He will never leave or forsake us. Advent reminds us that God's presence is not seasonal. Emmanuel did not come and go. His name remains His nature—God *with* us, always.

Daily Affirmation

Jesus is my Emmanuel. He is with me in every moment, every season, and every circumstance.

Prayer

Emmanuel, thank You for drawing near. You are not a distant God, but one who stepped into our world to redeem it. Teach me to recognize Your presence in the ordinary places of my life. When I feel alone, remind me that You are closer than my breath. Fill my heart with gratitude for the gift of Your nearness and help me carry that awareness into each day. Amen.

Journaling Prompt

- Where have you recently seen evidence of God's presence in your life?
- What situations make it most difficult for you to sense that He is near?
- Write a short prayer of thanks for specific moments when you felt Emmanuel's presence this year.

Verse to Write

"And surely I am with you always, to the very end of the age."
— *Matthew 28:20 (NIV)*

Reflection Break

When you decorate your Christmas tree today, whisper His name—Emmanuel. Sit quietly for a few moments and thank God for His nearness. Let His presence bring peace to your waiting and warmth to your worship.

December 6

The Word

Scripture Focus

"In the beginning was the Word, and the Word was with God, and the Word was God.

He was with God in the beginning.

Through him all things were made; without him nothing was made that has been made.

The Word became flesh and made his dwelling among us.

We have seen his glory, the glory of the one and only Son, who came from the Father, full of grace and truth."

— John 1:1–3, 14 (NIV)

Reflection

Before the manger, before the prophets, before the dawn of time itself—there was the Word. John opens his Gospel with a truth that bends the mind and stirs the heart: Jesus was not merely born in Bethlehem; He existed from eternity as the living Word of God.

In the Greek, John calls Him *Logos (Word)*. To the ancient world, that term carried weight. The *Logos* was understood as the divine reason or wisdom that ordered the universe. John takes that familiar idea and gives it breathtaking clarity: the divine *Word* is not an abstract force but a person. The Creator has a face and a name.

"The Word became flesh." These five words capture the wonder of Christmas. God did not shout His love from the heavens; He embodied it on earth. The invisible became visible. The eternal stepped into time. The all-powerful took on the vulnerability of human skin and bone.

Every miracle, every teaching, every act of compassion in Jesus' ministry flowed from that truth. The Word that once commanded light to burst into darkness now walked among us as the Light of the world. The same voice that spoke galaxies into motion now spoke forgiveness, healing, and hope.

John writes that the Word "made his dwelling among us," echoing the Old Testament image of God's presence dwelling in the tabernacle. The Greek for tabernacle literally means "tent" or "dwelling place." Jesus, the living Word, became God's dwelling place on earth. No longer confined to a temple, God's glory now walked the dusty roads of Galilee and entered human hearts. To behold Jesus is to see the glory of God revealed in grace and truth. Grace that welcomes the sinner. Truth that sets the captive free. Through Him, God's heart speaks clearly and tenderly: *You are seen. You are loved. You are Mine.*

As you reflect this Advent, remember that the Word who spoke creation into being still speaks today. His Word brings light to confusion, strength to weakness, and peace to the restless soul. Listen closely. The same Word that became flesh longs to dwell richly in you.

Daily Affirmation

Jesus is the Word made flesh. He reveals God's truth and grace to my heart and walks with me through every moment.

Prayer

Word made flesh, thank You for stepping into our world and revealing the Father's heart. Your words bring hope where there is despair and clarity where there is confusion. Teach me to treasure Your Word and to hear Your voice through Scripture and prayer. Let Your truth shape my thoughts and Your grace fill my speech. Dwell in me richly, Lord, as You once dwelt among us. Amen.

Journaling Prompt

- What does it mean to you that Jesus is both fully God and fully human?
- When has Scripture or God's Word spoken directly into your situation?
- Write about a time you experienced His presence through His Word.

Verse to Write

> *"The grass withers and the flowers fall, but the word of*
> *our God endures forever."*
> — *Isaiah 40:8 (NIV)*

Reflection Break

Before writing your Christmas cards, read John 1 aloud. Let the power of those opening words settle deeply in your spirit. The Word who created all things now lives within you.

December 7

The Lamb of God

Scripture Focus

> *"The next day John saw Jesus coming toward him and said,*
>
> *'Look, the Lamb of God, who takes away the sin of the world!'"*
>
> — *John 1:29 (NIV)*

Reflection

When John the Baptist first saw Jesus walking toward him at the Jordan River, his declaration must have stunned the crowd. Israel had waited centuries for a warrior-king to overthrow their oppressors, but John pointed to a carpenter's son and called Him *the Lamb of God*.

The phrase was more than symbolic—it was steeped in centuries of worship and sacrifice. Since the days of Moses, the people of Israel had offered spotless lambs as substitutes for their sins. Every sacrifice was a shadow of something greater, a foreshadowing of a perfect sacrifice still to come. At the first Passover, God instructed His people to place the blood of a lamb on their doorposts so that death would "pass over" them. In the wilderness, lambs were offered daily in the tabernacle to atone for sin. Yet none of those sacrifices could truly remove guilt and fully reconcile us to our Creator; they only pointed forward to the One who could.

When John called Jesus "the Lamb of God," he was proclaiming that the final sacrifice had arrived. Jesus was not only sinless— He was willing. He would take upon Himself the weight of every sin ever committed and offer His life in exchange for ours. Isaiah had prophesied it long before: "He was led like a lamb to the slaughter, and as a sheep before its shearers is silent, so he did not open his mouth" (Isaiah 53:7).

At the cross, the symbolism of the lamb met its fulfillment. The blood that once covered doorposts now covered souls. The judgment that once passed over homes now passed over hearts. Jesus became the Passover Lamb for all time. But the story does not end in death. In Revelation, John sees the risen Christ still described as *"a Lamb, looking as if it had been slain"*—alive, reigning, victorious. Heaven's throne is not occupied by a warrior dripping with conquest, but by a Lamb whose power is love and whose victory is redemption.

As you reflect today, remember that the Lamb of God not only forgives you; He restores you. His blood covers guilt, shame, and fear. It declares you free.

Daily Affirmation

Jesus is the Lamb of God. His sacrifice covers my sin and restores me to the Father in perfect love.

Prayer

Lamb of God, thank You for bearing my sin and taking my place. Your mercy is beyond measure. Help me never to treat Your sacrifice lightly. Teach me to live each day in gratitude and humility, knowing that I am forgiven and made new through Your blood. May my life be a reflection of Your grace. Amen.

Journaling Prompt

- What emotions or thoughts come to mind when you consider Jesus as the Lamb of God?
- How has His sacrifice changed the way you see yourself and others?
- Write a prayer of thanksgiving for the forgiveness and freedom you have in Christ.

Verse to Write

> *"For you know that it was not with perishable things such as silver or gold that you were redeemed, but with the precious blood of Christ, a lamb without blemish or defect."*
> — *1 Peter 1:18–19 (NIV)*

Reflection Break

Take five quiet minutes to thank Jesus for the price He paid for your freedom. Write a short note or prayer of gratitude in the margin of your Bible or on a slip of paper and keep it somewhere visible today as a reminder that you are redeemed.

December 8

The Good Shepherd

Scripture Focus

"I am the good shepherd. The good shepherd lays down his life for the sheep."
— *John 10:11 (NIV)*

Reflection

Throughout Scripture, God often compares His people to sheep. It is not a flattering image. Sheep are easily distracted, easily frightened, and quick to wander away from safety. Yet that imagery reveals something important about the heart of God: He does not reject the distracted, the frightened, or the wandering—He rescues them.

In the ancient world, shepherds lived among their flocks. They led them to pasture by day, protected them through the night, and risked their lives to guard them from danger. It was hard, humble work. When Jesus called Himself the *Good Shepherd*, He claimed a role of both authority and intimacy. He was not a hired hand who fled when trouble came; He was the One willing to lay down His life to save His sheep.

The people listening that day would have remembered Psalm 23: "The Lord is my shepherd; I lack nothing." For centuries, Israel had known God as their Shepherd, but in Jesus, that promise took on flesh. He knew every voice in His flock, and His own voice could calm fear with a single word. He called each sheep by name, just as He calls you.

When Jesus described Himself as "the Good Shepherd," He contrasted His heart with false leaders who exploited the flock. His care is personal and sacrificial. He doesn't drive His sheep from behind; He leads them from the front, going before them into every valley and over every hill. At Christmas, we often picture Jesus as a baby in a manger, but that manger was the resting place of the Shepherd who would one day carry a cross. His birth and His sacrifice are woven together by love that never lets go.

As you move through this Advent season, remember that your Good Shepherd is near. He is guiding your steps even when you feel unsure. His voice cuts through the noise and reminds you that you belong to Him. The same hands that once held a shepherd's staff now hold you securely in grace. You are seen. You are known. You are safe.

Daily Affirmation

Jesus is my Good Shepherd. He knows my name, guides my steps, and never leaves me lost or alone.

Prayer

Good Shepherd, thank You for knowing me so personally and loving me so faithfully. When I wander, call me back. When I fear, calm me with Your presence. Help me recognize Your voice above all others. Teach me to trust that wherever You lead, it is for my good and Your glory. Amen.

Journaling Prompt

- What does it mean to you that Jesus knows your name and cares about your individual journey?
- Have you ever experienced His gentle leading during a difficult time?
- Write about a time when you felt lost and how God guided you back to peace.

Verse to Write

"He tends his flock like a shepherd: He gathers the lambs in his arms and carries them close to his heart;
he gently leads those that have young."
— *Isaiah 40:11 (NIV)*

Reflection Break

As you bake cookies or complete another Christmas activity today, pause for a moment. Whisper a prayer of thanks that the Good Shepherd walks beside you through both quiet and chaos. Let His nearness steady your heart today.

December 9

The Light of the World

Scripture Focus

"When Jesus spoke again to the people, he said,
  'I am the light of the world. Whoever follows me will
never walk in darkness, but will have the light of life.'"
  — John 8:12 (NIV)

Reflection

D arkness is not only the absence of light; it is the absence of direction. In the dark, everything feels uncertain—where to step, what lies ahead, how to find our way back. Humanity has wrestled with this kind of darkness since Eden, when sin cast its long shadow over creation. Yet in the midst of that shadow, God promised that light would come.

When Jesus declared, "I am the light of the world," He was standing in the temple courts during the Festival of Tabernacles.

Massive golden lamps illuminated the night, celebrating how God had led Israel through the wilderness with a pillar of fire. Against that brilliant backdrop, Jesus made a radical claim: the same divine light that once guided their ancestors now stood among them in human form.

Light does what nothing else can—it reveals, it warms, it gives life. Jesus, the true Light, exposes what is hidden, not to condemn but to redeem. His light reaches into the corners of the soul that shame and fear try to keep hidden. No darkness is too deep for Him to overcome.

The world offers many false lights, temporary glows of distraction, comfort, or success, but only Christ gives light that endures. His light doesn't flicker when the winds of hardship blow. It remains steady, even in grief, uncertainty, or loss. As you move through Advent, pay attention to the lights around you: the soft glow of candles in the window, the sparkle of ornaments on the tree, the glimmer of stars on a cold night. Each one is a faint echo of the true Light that entered our world at Christmas.

When you hang a string of lights this season or drive past homes aglow in the dark, let it remind you that the Light of the World still shines in the darkness of every heart and every home. And as His followers, we are called to reflect that light—to bring warmth and hope to those around us who are still searching for their way.

Darkness has no defense against light. When Jesus enters a life, the shadows scatter.

Daily Affirmation

Jesus is the Light of the World. His presence guides me, His truth reveals my path, and His love drives out my fear.

Prayer

Light of the World, thank You for breaking through my darkness with Your truth and grace. Shine in the hidden places of my heart and drive out every shadow of fear, doubt, and shame. Help me reflect Your light in my words and actions so that others may see Your glory through me. Amen.

Journaling Prompt

- Where in your life do you need the light of Christ to shine right now?
- Who around you needs to experience His light through your kindness or encouragement?
- Write a short prayer asking God to help you reflect His light to someone this week.

Verse to Write

"The light shines in the darkness, and the darkness has not overcome it."
  — *John 1:5 (NIV)*

Reflection Break

As you plug in the Christmas tree lights or see a neighborhood home glowing against the night, pause and thank God that His light still shines. Whisper a prayer: "Jesus, be my light." Let that simple sentence guide you through the week.

December 10

The Bread of Life

Scripture Focus

> *"Then Jesus declared, 'I am the bread of life. Whoever comes to me will never go hungry, and whoever believes in me will never be thirsty.'"*
> — *John 6:35 (NIV)*

Reflection

Few things feel more comforting or familiar than the smell of freshly baked bread. It fills a home with warmth and promises nourishment. Throughout Scripture, bread represents God's provision—first in the manna that sustained Israel in the wilderness (*Exodus*), and later in the Passover bread that reminded them of His deliverance.

When Jesus called Himself the *Bread of Life*, He was speaking to a crowd that had just witnessed Him miraculously feed more than five thousand people. They followed Him, hoping for another meal. But Jesus offered them something far greater: not bread that satisfies for a day, but life that satisfies forever.

His words reached back to the wilderness wanderings of their ancestors. The manna that fell from heaven met physical hunger, but it could not give eternal life. Every morning, the Israelites had to gather more for that day's physical nourishment. In contrast, Jesus promised that whoever came to Him would never hunger again, because He alone could fill the deepest emptiness of the human heart.

In every age, people search for satisfaction—through success, relationships, possessions, or experiences—but nothing apart from Christ can truly nourish the soul. He alone sustains. He alone satisfies.

The bread Jesus spoke of was also sacrificial. Later in John's Gospel, He said, "The bread that I will give for the life of the world is my flesh." His body would be broken so that ours might be made whole. Each time we take communion, we remember that holy exchange—the Bread of Heaven given for us.

So much of Advent invites us to wait with hope, but this name reminds us to receive with gratitude. Christ does not offer us crumbs of comfort; He gives us Himself. Every longing finds its fulfillment in Him. As you break bread this season—whether at the dinner table, a Christmas party, or while baking loaves to share with friends—let the act remind you of the One who came to feed every hungry heart and soul with grace and truth.

Daily Affirmation

Jesus is the Bread of Life. He fills my soul with His presence and satisfies every hunger within me.

Prayer

Bread of Heaven, thank You for being my true nourishment. I come to You today with open hands and a hungry heart. Feed me with Your Word and fill me with Your peace. Help me find my satisfaction in You alone. May I share Your love generously, offering the bread of grace to others. Amen.

Journaling Prompt

- What "hungers" in your life have you tried to fill apart from Christ?
- How does knowing Jesus as the Bread of Life change your perspective on contentment?
- Write a prayer of gratitude for how God has provided for your needs this season.

Verse to Write

"Man shall not live on bread alone, but on every word that comes from the mouth of God."
  — Matthew 4:4 (NIV)

Reflection Break

During Advent, our homes often overflow with food, sweets, and gatherings around the table. Yet even in the midst of abundance, our hearts can feel hungry for something more. When you prepare or share a meal today, pause to remember that the Bread of Life offers nourishment that never runs out. Take a moment to thank God for His faithful provision. Pray for someone you know who feels spiritually empty, and ask the Lord to satisfy their heart with His presence.

December 11

The Way, The Truth, and The Life

Scripture Focus

"Jesus answered, 'I am the way and the truth and the life.

No one comes to the Father except through me.'"

— John 14:6 (NIV)

Reflection

These words were spoken on the eve of Jesus' crucifixion. The disciples were troubled and confused. Their teacher had washed their feet, predicted His death, and told them He was going away. Thomas voiced what everyone felt: "Lord, we don't know where you are going, so how can we know the way?" Jesus' response reached beyond that moment: "I am the way and the truth and the life." He wasn't offering a set of directions or another philosophy. He was declaring Himself the destination, the guide, and the means by which we arrive.

Each phrase carries weight.

He is *the Way*—the only path to the Father. Religion and moral effort can't bridge the gap between humanity and heaven, but Jesus can. Through His death and resurrection, He opened the road home for every wandering heart.

He is *the Truth*—not just a teacher of truth, but Truth embodied. In a world where opinions shift like sand, Jesus stands unchanging. His words don't adjust to culture or convenience. They reveal the heart of God and anchor ours when uncertainty surrounds us.

He is *the Life*—the source and sustainer of all that is good. Apart from Him, our souls grow restless and empty. Through Him, we find renewal, joy, and peace that last beyond this world.

Advent calls us to reflect on that truth. The baby in the manger is not one of many ways; He is *the* Way. He doesn't simply show what is true; He *is* Truth. And He doesn't just grant life; He *is* Life itself. During this season, our calendars fill quickly, and we often find ourselves pulled in every direction—shopping lists, gatherings, travel, and family traditions. Yet in the middle of it all, Jesus invites us to pause and remember the simplicity of His promise. When we don't know which path to take or how to make sense of what's ahead, He gently reminds us: "Follow Me."

When you drive home through Christmas lights this week or sit quietly after a long day, let those moments turn your heart toward the One who lights the way. His truth steadies every step, and His life gives meaning to every mile. Following Him may not always be the easiest route, but it will always lead you home.

Daily Affirmation

Jesus is the Way, the Truth, and the Life. He leads me to the Father, fills me with truth, and gives me everlasting life.

Prayer

Lord Jesus, thank You for showing me the way to the Father through Your grace. When I am uncertain, remind me that Your truth never changes. When I feel lost, lead me back to Your path. Teach me to walk in step with You, to speak truth with love, and to live in the fullness of Your life each day. Amen.

Journaling Prompt

- What area of your life feels uncertain or directionless right now?
- How can you choose to follow Jesus as "the Way" instead of relying on your own understanding?
- Write a reflection on how His truth has brought light or conviction to your heart recently.

Verse to Write

> *"Your word is a lamp for my feet, a light on my path."*
> *— Psalm 119:105 (NIV)*

Reflection Break

Take a short walk outside tonight or sit quietly near your Christmas tree lights. As you notice each small light breaking the darkness, thank Jesus for being your Way, your Truth, and your Life. Ask Him to guide your next step and fill you with peace.

December 12

The True Vine

Scripture Focus

"I am the true vine, and my Father is the gardener.
He cuts off every branch in me that bears no fruit, while
every branch that does bear fruit he prunes so that it will
be even more fruitful."
— John 15:1–2 (NIV)

Reflection

In the vineyards of ancient Israel, grapevines symbolized abundance and blessing. They were also a familiar image for God's people. Again and again, the Old Testament described Israel as the vine that God planted, tended, and longed to see bear fruit. Yet the nation often turned away, producing bitterness instead of sweetness. By saying, "I am the true vine," Jesus fulfilled what Israel's story foreshadowed. He alone produces the kind of fruit that glorifies God. Everyone who believes in Him becomes part of that living vine, nourished by His life and sustained by His Spirit.

This passage also contains a gentle warning: fruitful branches must remain connected to the vine. Apart from Him, there is no growth, no strength, no lasting fruit. The Christian life isn't about striving harder but abiding deeper. Jesus explained that the Father, the Gardener, lovingly prunes every branch that bears fruit. The process may be painful, but pruning is never punishment—it's preparation. Cutting away what hinders growth allows new fruit to flourish.

As you think about this truth during Advent, consider how many things compete for your attention: shopping lists, schedules, and social commitments. It's easy to become tangled in busy branches that produce more exhaustion than fruit. The season of Advent calls us back to abiding—staying rooted in the One who gives life.

Perhaps while you decorate your home, hang garland, or set the table for guests, you notice the intertwining of branches and greenery. Let those simple touches remind you of the vine that sustains you. Every moment spent in His presence, every prayer whispered in faith, strengthens your connection to Him.

The fruit that grows from abiding is not measured by productivity or perfection but by love, joy, peace, patience, kindness, goodness, faithfulness, gentleness, and self-control. These are the gifts that ripen quietly in hearts that stay close to Christ.

Advent invites us to slow down, remain in His love, and let His life flow through ours. The True Vine doesn't demand performance; He offers partnership. His strength becomes our supply. His life becomes our own.

Daily Affirmation

Jesus is the True Vine. I will remain in Him, trusting His life to bear fruit through me.

Prayer

True Vine, thank You for giving me a place to belong. Help me stay connected to You when distractions pull me away. Teach me to welcome Your pruning as a gift that brings growth. Let Your Spirit produce lasting fruit in my heart and in every relationship I touch. May my life reflect the beauty of abiding in You. Amen.

Journaling Prompt

- What "branches" in your life might God be pruning right now to make room for new growth?
- How do you experience the difference between striving and abiding?
- Write a short prayer asking God to help you stay connected to Him during this season.

Verse to Write

> *"Remain in me, as I also remain in you.*
> *No branch can bear fruit by itself; it must remain in the vine.*
> *Neither can you bear fruit unless you remain in me."*
> *— John 15:4 (NIV)*

Reflection Break

While arranging greenery or trimming your Christmas tree, pause and look at the branches. Thank Jesus for being your source of life. Ask Him to help you remain rooted in His presence and to make your life fruitful in ways that honor Him.

December 13

The Son of Man

Scripture Focus

> *"For even the Son of Man did not come to be served, but to serve, and to give his life as a ransom for many."*
> — *Mark 10:45 (NIV)*

Reflection

Of all the titles Jesus used to describe Himself, *Son of Man* was His favorite. It appears more than eighty times in the Gospels. At first, it sounds ordinary—after all, we're all sons and daughters of humanity—but in Scripture, this phrase carries deep meaning and mystery.

The title comes from the prophet Daniel's vision centuries before Christ's birth. Daniel saw "one like a son of man, coming with the clouds of heaven," who was given everlasting dominion and glory (Daniel 7:13–14). The Jews understood this to refer to the coming Messiah, a divine ruler who would reign forever. When Jesus called Himself the *Son of Man*, He was identifying Himself as that promised figure, the one with authority from heaven. Yet, He also embraced the full humanity that title implied.

The beauty of this name lies in its balance. Jesus is both divine and human, majestic and humble. He has all authority, yet He chose to serve. He holds the power of heaven, yet He washed the feet of His friends. He could have commanded angels, but instead, He carried a cross.

In Mark 10:45, Jesus turns the world's idea of greatness upside down. True leadership is not about status but sacrifice. True power is shown through humility. The *Son of Man* came not to be waited on but to pour Himself out for others. Advent reminds us that God's glory came wrapped in humanity. The One who set the stars in place also knew the ache of tired feet and the sting of betrayal. He became like us so that we could become like Him.

As you move through this week of Advent—perhaps while standing in line at a store, delivering cookies to a neighbor, or tidying up your home—remember that serving others is not a small task. It is a reflection of the heart of Christ. Each act of kindness, each moment of patience, mirrors the humility of the Son of Man who came to serve.

He still does. Every day, He intercedes for us before the Father, guides us through the Spirit, and meets us in the ordinary moments where heaven touches earth. The Son of Man has not come to be served, but to serve—and His hands are still extended toward us.

Daily Affirmation

Jesus is the Son of Man. He understands my humanity and teaches me to live with humility and love.

Prayer

Son of Man, thank You for stepping into our world with compassion and humility. You understand what it means to be human. Help me follow Your example by serving others with grace and gentleness. When pride or selfishness rises in me, remind me that greatness is found in love. Amen.

Journaling Prompt

- What does it mean to you that Jesus understands every human experience, including weakness and weariness?
- How can you reflect His servant-hearted nature this week?
- Write about one way you can serve someone quietly, without recognition, as an act of worship.

Verse to Write

> *"In your relationships with one another, have the same mindset as Christ Jesus:*
> *who, being in very nature God, did not consider equality with God something to be used to his own advantage;*
> *rather, he made himself nothing by taking the very nature of a servant."*

— *Philippians 2:5–7 (NIV)*

Reflection Break

As you serve others today—whether preparing a meal, running errands, or offering help—whisper a simple prayer: "Jesus, teach me to serve like You." Let every act of love become an offering of gratitude to the One who came not to be served, but to serve.

December 14

The Great High Priest

Scripture Focus

"Therefore, since we have a great high priest who has ascended into heaven, Jesus the Son of God, let us hold firmly to the faith we profess. For we do not have a high priest who is unable to empathize with our weaknesses, but we have one who has been tempted in every way, just as we are—yet he did not sin."
— Hebrews 4:14–15 (NIV)

Reflection

In ancient Israel, the high priest held a sacred and solemn role. Once a year, on the Day of Atonement, he entered the Holy of Holies to offer a sacrifice for the sins of the people. The ritual was so holy that a rope was tied around his ankle in case he did not survive the presence of God's glory. Only the high priest could stand before God as mediator for the nation.

But the book of Hebrews tells us that Jesus is the *Great* High Priest — not one who enters a man-made temple, but heaven itself. He doesn't offer the blood of animals but His own. His sacrifice was perfect, final, and eternal. The curtain that once separated humanity from God was torn in two. Because of Him, the way is open for all who believe.

This name reminds us that Jesus is both our mediator and our mercy. He stands between heaven and earth, bridging the gap that sin created. Yet He also draws near to us with understanding and compassion. Unlike earthly priests, He doesn't need to offer sacrifices for His own sin, because He is sinless. But He does understand our weaknesses. He walked this earth, faced temptation, felt exhaustion, and knew sorrow.

When you bring your prayers to Him, you are not speaking into empty air. You are speaking to the One who knows what it means to be human. He knows the weight of grief, the ache of loss, and the sting of betrayal. He knows how heavy it can be to wait for God's timing. And because He knows, He can help.

During Advent, when our days fill quickly with tasks and expectations, it's easy to forget that prayer is not a ritual but a relationship. Your Great High Priest welcomes you into God's presence with confidence and grace. You don't need to earn the right to come near; the invitation has already been signed in His blood.

As you pause for a moment of quiet tonight, let this name settle into your heart: *Jesus, my Great High Priest.* He intercedes for you even now, lifting your needs to the Father with love that never tires. Because of Him, you can come boldly before the throne of grace — not in fear, but in faith.

Daily Affirmation

Jesus is my Great High Priest. He understands my weakness, intercedes for me, and welcomes me into God's presence.

Prayer

Great High Priest, thank You for standing in the gap between heaven and earth for me. You know my struggles and still call me Your own. When I feel unworthy, remind me that Your blood has made me clean. When I grow weary, lift my heart through Your intercession. Teach me to draw near with confidence, trusting the mercy You have already secured. Amen.

Journaling Prompt

- How does it change your prayer life to know that Jesus intercedes for you?
- When have you experienced His compassion and understanding in a moment of weakness?
- Write a short prayer of gratitude for the access you have to God through Christ.

Verse to Write

> "Let us then approach God's throne of grace with confidence,
>   so that we may receive mercy and find grace to help us

in our time of need."
  — Hebrews 4:16 (NIV)

Reflection Break

Before you go to bed tonight, spend a few quiet minutes in prayer. Picture yourself stepping into the presence of God, confident and unafraid. Thank Jesus, your Great High Priest, for making that access possible and for praying over you even now.

December 15

The Healer

Scripture Focus

"But he was pierced for our transgressions, he was crushed for our iniquities;
the punishment that brought us peace was on him, and by his wounds we are healed."
— Isaiah 53:5 (NIV)

Reflection

The ache of waiting for healing can be one of life's heaviest burdens. It's a quiet pain that doesn't always show on the surface. For some, it's the weariness of chronic illness. For others, it's watching someone they love suffer. Advent meets us in that tension — the space between hope and fulfillment, between prayer and answer.

Isaiah's prophecy points us to a kind of healing that runs deeper than we often imagine. When he wrote, "By his wounds we are healed," he spoke not only of physical restoration but of the healing of the soul — the mending of what sin had broken. Jesus' ministry reflected that truth. He touched lepers no one else would approach. He gave sight to the blind, raised the dead, and comforted the brokenhearted. Every miracle whispered the same promise: the curse is being undone.

Yet not everyone in Scripture who asked for healing received it immediately. Paul pleaded three times for God to remove his "thorn in the flesh," and God answered, "My grace is sufficient for you." Even Lazarus, raised from the grave, would one day face death again. These moments remind us that divine healing is not always instantaneous, but it is always certain — if not now, then in eternity.

Jesus is the Healer because His power reaches beyond symptoms to the root of suffering itself. On the cross, He bore our sin, sorrow, and pain. His resurrection guarantees that sickness and death will not have the final word. One day, every body will be whole, every tear wiped away, and every story of pain rewritten by glory.

Until then, He walks beside us in the waiting. He strengthens weary bodies, renews faltering faith, and holds trembling hands with compassion that does not fail. His presence is healing even when the pain remains. This Advent, when you sit beside someone who is sick, wait in a doctor's office, or take your own medicine with a sigh, remember that your Healer sees you. He is near to the brokenhearted and faithful in every valley.

Perhaps as you prepare a warm meal for your family, care for someone in need, or simply rest under a soft blanket on a cold day, breathe this prayer: "Lord, heal what only You can." Trust that He is working in ways seen and unseen. His timing is perfect, and His love is complete.

Daily Affirmation

Jesus is my Healer. His presence brings peace to my pain, hope to my waiting, and strength to my soul.

Prayer

Healer of hearts and bodies, thank You for understanding suffering and meeting me in it. When I am weary, lift my eyes to Your faithfulness. When pain feels endless, remind me of the day when all things will be made new. I trust You with my health, my family, and my future. Heal me in Your perfect way — body, mind, and spirit — and help me rest in Your love. Amen.

Journaling Prompt

- Where in your life are you praying for healing right now?
- How have you seen God's presence bring comfort or strength, even when healing hasn't come yet?
- Write a letter of gratitude to Jesus, thanking Him for walking with you through your pain.

Verse to Write

> *"Praise the Lord, my soul, and forget not all his benefits*
> *—*
>
> *who forgives all your sins and heals all your diseases."*
> *— Psalm 103:2–3 (NIV)*

Reflection Break

Take a few minutes today to rest quietly. Play soft worship music, Christmas music, or sit in stillness. Invite Jesus, the Healer, to meet you in your weariness. Thank Him for what He has already restored and trust Him for what He is still mending.

December 16

The Bridegroom

Scripture Focus

"The bride belongs to the bridegroom. The friend who
attends the bridegroom waits and listens for him, and is
full of joy when he hears the bridegroom's voice."
— *John 3:29 (NIV)*

Reflection

All through Scripture, God uses the language of covenant love to describe His relationship with His people. From the prophets to Revelation, the imagery of marriage appears again and again — not as sentiment, but as sacred promise. When Jesus called Himself the *Bridegroom*, He was declaring that God's long-promised union with His people had come near.

In ancient Jewish tradition, a bridegroom left his father's house to prepare a home for his bride. When everything was ready, he returned — often at night, accompanied by friends and lamps — to bring her home for the wedding celebration. Jesus used that same imagery to describe His mission. He left His Father's house, came to claim His bride through the cross, and promised to return when the dwelling place He prepares for us is complete. John the Baptist, who called himself "the friend of the bridegroom," understood this joy. His role was to prepare the way, to announce that the long wait was over. The Bridegroom had come.

Throughout His ministry, Jesus spoke of this relationship with tenderness. He referred to Himself as the Bridegroom when questioned about fasting, hinting that His disciples' joy came from His presence. Later, Paul would write that the church is the bride of Christ, loved with a self-sacrificing devotion that cleanses, redeems, and restores (Ephesians 5:25–27).

Advent invites us to remember not only that Christ came, but that He is coming again. We live in that sacred in-between, waiting for the final celebration — the marriage supper of the Lamb. Every candlelit service, every Christmas feast, every moment of worship gives us a small taste of that future joy.

Today, imagine the greater celebration that awaits. The Bridegroom has not forgotten His promise. He is preparing a place where sorrow will end, joy will be full, and love will never fade. While we wait, He invites us to live as a faithful bride — watchful, hopeful, adorned in the beauty of holiness. Not striving for perfection, but resting in belonging. Our preparation is not anxious but joyful, because the One who promised to return is faithful.

Daily Affirmation

Jesus is my Bridegroom. He loves me completely, prepares a place for me, and will return to bring me home.

Prayer

Faithful Bridegroom, thank You for Your steadfast love. You have chosen me, redeemed me, and promised to return. Teach me to wait with anticipation rather than fear. Fill my heart with joy as I prepare for the day I will see You face to face. Let my life reflect the beauty of Your faithfulness and love. Amen.

Journaling Prompt

- What does it mean to you personally that Jesus calls Himself the Bridegroom?
- How can you live with hopeful expectancy while you wait for His return?
- Write a short reflection on how His love has changed the way you see yourself.

Verse to Write

"Let us rejoice and be glad and give him glory!
  For the wedding of the Lamb has come, and his bride has made herself ready."
  — Revelation 19:7 (NIV)

Reflection Break

As you prepare your home or share a meal with loved ones, pause to picture the joy of the wedding feast to come. Whisper a prayer of gratitude to your Bridegroom for His unwavering love and for the promise that He will one day make all things new.

December 17

The Cornerstone

Scripture Focus

"Consequently, you are no longer foreigners and strangers,
    but fellow citizens with God's people and also members of his household,
    built on the foundation of the apostles and prophets,
    with Christ Jesus himself as the chief cornerstone."
    — Ephesians 2:19–20 (NIV)

Reflection

In ancient construction, the cornerstone was the most important stone in the foundation. It was placed first, and every other stone aligned with it. If the cornerstone was crooked, the whole building would be unstable. When Scripture calls Jesus the *Cornerstone*, it means He is both the foundation and the standard for all who belong to Him.

The prophets spoke of this long before His birth. Isaiah declared, "See, I lay a stone in Zion, a tested stone, a precious cornerstone for a sure foundation" (Isaiah 28:16). Centuries later, Peter would quote that same verse, explaining that while some reject the stone, for those who believe, it becomes the secure foundation of faith.

Advent invites us to reflect on what our lives are built upon. The holidays can sometimes reveal how shaky our foundations are — stress, comparison, or grief can expose the cracks. Yet Jesus, the Cornerstone, remains steady. He holds us together when everything else feels uncertain. As Paul wrote, we are no longer strangers or outsiders. Through Christ, we have become part of God's household, joined together into something strong and lasting. Each believer is a living stone fitted into His spiritual structure. Our differences don't weaken the building; they make it beautiful.

When Jesus entered the world as a baby, He came to rebuild what sin had fractured. On the cross, He bore the weight of all that was broken, and through His resurrection, He became the foundation of a new creation. He is the sure footing for every believer who trusts in Him. This season, as you hang stockings, decorate your home, or build a gingerbread house with loved ones, consider what it means to build your life on Christ. He is the alignment point for every dream, decision, and relationship. When your thoughts and choices line up with Him, your foundation is secure.

Storms may come, but the Cornerstone does not shift. The winds of culture may change, but His truth remains unmoved. Those who build on Him will never be put to shame.

Daily Affirmation

Jesus is my Cornerstone. My life is built on His truth, sustained by His strength, and aligned with His will.

Prayer

Cornerstone of my faith, thank You for being the firm foundation I can always depend on. When life feels unstable, remind me that You are unshakable. Help me build every part of my life on Your Word and align my heart with Your truth. May I stand strong in faith and become a living stone that reflects Your glory. Amen.

Journaling Prompt

- What areas of your life feel shaky or uncertain right now?
- How can you realign those areas with the truth of Christ as your Cornerstone?
- Write about a time when God's stability carried you through instability.

Verse to Write

> *"Therefore this is what the Sovereign Lord says:*
> *'See, I lay a stone in Zion, a tested stone, a precious cornerstone for a sure foundation;*
> *the one who relies on it will never be stricken with panic.'"*

— Isaiah 28:16 (NIV)

Reflection Break

While decorating your home or finishing a Christmas project, pause and thank Jesus for being your sure foundation. Ask Him to steady your heart and help you build everything you do this season on His truth and love.

December 18

The Lion of Judah

Scripture Focus

> *"Then one of the elders said to me, 'Do not weep!*
> *See, the Lion of the tribe of Judah, the Root of David,*
> *has triumphed.*
> *He is able to open the scroll and its seven seals.'"*
> *— Revelation 5:5 (NIV)*

Reflection

In the final book of the Bible, Revelation, the apostle John describes a vision that takes his breath away. Heaven stands still. A sealed scroll lies in God's hand, and no one is found worthy to open it. John begins to weep — until one of the elders touches his shoulder and says, "Do not weep! The Lion of the tribe of Judah has triumphed."

The title *Lion of Judah* stretches all the way back to Genesis, where Jacob blessed his son Judah, saying, "You are a lion's cub; the scepter will not depart from Judah" (Genesis 49:9–10). From that tribe would come the Messiah — a ruler fierce in righteousness and mighty in victory.

When John turns to see the lion, he expects power and dominance. Instead, he sees a Lamb, standing as though slain. In that single moment, heaven reveals the mystery of God's strength. The Lion conquered not through force but through sacrifice. His roar shook the gates of hell, and His blood silenced the power of sin. The Lion of Judah embodies both majesty and mercy. He is fierce against evil but tender toward His own. His strength defends, restores, and redeems. For those who belong to Him, His victory is not distant history — it's present reality.

Advent often centers on quiet scenes: the manger, the shepherds, the gentle light of a star. Yet the baby lying in the straw was and is the Lion of Judah. His birth declared war on darkness. Each miracle of His ministry, each word of truth He spoke, was a roar that shattered lies and called the lost home. As you prepare for Christmas, remember that the story of Bethlehem does not end with soft lullabies. It leads to resurrection power and everlasting triumph. The same Jesus who came humbly now reigns gloriously. One day He will return, not as a fragile infant, but as the victorious King whose rule will never end.

When you hear the swelling notes of a favorite Christmas hymn, or when you feel courage rise where fear once lived, let it remind you that the Lion still reigns. His roar still echoes through every believer who stands firm in faith. If you are walking through a battle right now — spiritual, emotional, or physical — take heart. The Lion of Judah has already overcome.

Daily Affirmation

Jesus is the Lion of Judah. His victory is my confidence, His power my protection, and His reign my peace.

Prayer

Lion of Judah, thank You for conquering sin and death with Your strength and love. When I feel weak, remind me that Your victory stands secure. Give me courage to face every challenge knowing You fight for me. Let my life declare Your power and my heart rest in Your triumph. Amen.

Journaling Prompt

- What battle are you facing today that needs the courage of the Lion of Judah?
- How does it encourage you to know that Jesus has already triumphed over every enemy?
- Write a prayer declaring His authority over fear, sin, or discouragement in your life.

Verse to Write

> "They will wage war against the Lamb, but the Lamb will triumph over them because he is Lord of lords and King of kings — and with him will be his called, chosen and faithful followers."
> — Revelation 17:14 (NIV)

Reflection Break

As you listen to Christmas music or light your tree tonight, think of the Lion of Judah — the mighty King who came as a Lamb. Whisper a prayer of courage: "Lord, help me live boldly in the victory You've already won."

December 19

The Resurrection and the Life

Scripture Focus

"Jesus said to her, 'I am the resurrection and the life.
The one who believes in me will live, even though they
die;
and whoever lives by believing in me will never die. Do
you believe this?'"
— John 11:25–26 (NIV)

Reflection

The scene in John 11 is one of the most intimate and powerful in the Gospels. Jesus arrives in Bethany to find His dear friend Lazarus already dead and buried. Martha runs to meet Him, grief pouring out through her words. "Lord, if you had been here, my brother would not have died." Her pain is familiar to anyone who has prayed for something that didn't happen, at least not in time. Yet what Jesus says next changes everything: "I am the resurrection and the life." Notice that He doesn't just *offer* resurrection — He *is* resurrection. The power to raise the dead is not something Jesus does; it is who He is. In Him, life itself has a name and a face.

Moments later, He calls Lazarus out of the tomb, proving that His authority reaches even into death. But this miracle pointed beyond that single grave to another — His own. The empty tomb on Easter morning was not only a victory for Christ; it was a victory for all who believe in Him. Advent prepares our hearts for Bethlehem, but it also points us toward the empty tomb. The baby born in the manger came to break the chains of death. The same voice that cried out in a stable would one day cry out from a cross, "It is finished." Through His death and resurrection, He turned mourning into dancing and fear into faith.

If you've ever walked through loss — a loved one, a dream, or a season of life — take comfort in this name. Jesus meets you right there, in the ache of absence, and speaks the same truth He spoke to Martha: "I am the resurrection and the life." Because of Him, death is not the end; it's a doorway. Because of Him, grief holds hope, and every goodbye whispered in faith becomes a promise of reunion.

This week, as you attend gatherings or decorate your home, you may find yourself thinking of those who are no longer at the table. Allow your sorrow to mingle with hope. The same Jesus who wept at Lazarus's tomb holds your tears and promises life beyond loss. When He returns, graves will open, tears will dry, and His people will rise. The Resurrection and the Life has already written the final chapter — and it ends in glory.

Daily Affirmation

Jesus is the Resurrection and the Life. In Him I have victory over death and the promise of eternal life.

Prayer

Resurrected Lord, thank You for bringing life out of what feels hopeless. When grief threatens to consume me, remind me of Your power and Your promises. Renew my faith to believe that nothing is beyond Your reach. Let Your resurrection life breathe fresh hope into my heart today. Amen.

Journaling Prompt

- How has the promise of resurrection brought comfort to you in times of loss?
- What areas of your life feel lifeless and need the renewing power of Christ today?
- Write a prayer of hope, thanking Jesus for conquering death and bringing eternal life.

Verse to Write

"Praise be to the God and Father of our Lord Jesus Christ!
In his great mercy he has given us new birth into a living hope
through the resurrection of Jesus Christ from the dead."
— 1 Peter 1:3 (NIV)

Reflection Break

Take a quiet moment tonight to remember loved ones who are with Jesus. Light a small candle or sit beneath twinkling Christmas lights and thank Him that death is not the end. Whisper His promise to your soul: "I am the resurrection and the life."

December 20

The Savior of the World

Scripture Focus

*"We have heard for ourselves, and we know that this man
really is the Savior of the world."*
  — John 4:42 (NIV)

Reflection

The title *Savior of the World* first appears on the lips of
unlikely witnesses — the people of a Samaritan village.
After Jesus met the woman at the well, her testimony
led her neighbors to hear Him for themselves. They came
skeptical but left convinced: this man was not just a teacher
or prophet. He was the Savior of the world. Those words carry
both wonder and weight. In Jesus' time, Jews and Samaritans
avoided one another. Yet salvation broke through those man-
made walls. The gospel has always crossed boundaries, reaching
every tribe, tongue, and nation.

To call Jesus *Savior* is to acknowledge both our need and His mercy. Humanity had no way to save itself. Sin fractured our relationship with God, leaving us lost and longing for redemption. But Jesus stepped into that gap — fully God, fully man — to accomplish what no one else could. He lived the life we could not live and died the death we deserved. His sacrifice was not limited to one people group or nation. It was for everyone who would believe. When John the Baptist saw Him and declared, "Behold, the Lamb of God who takes away the sin of the world," he echoed heaven's plan: a global redemption born in a humble manger.

The Christmas story is not just for a single time or place. It's for the entire world. The angels who announced His birth said their good news was for "all the people." The Savior who came for shepherds in the fields also came for kings in their palaces, for the broken and the searching, for you and for me.

As Advent draws nearer to Christmas morning, it's easy to focus on personal traditions — baking cookies, wrapping gifts, gathering with loved ones. Those moments are sacred, but they also remind us of something larger: the gift of salvation meant to be shared. The One born in Bethlehem didn't come to save a few; He came to redeem the world. If your heart feels heavy this season — burdened by the pain of a divided world or the sorrow of your own story — remember this: the Savior of the World still saves. His reach has not shortened. His grace has not weakened. His salvation still transforms hearts, one at a time.

Daily Affirmation

Jesus is the Savior of the World. His grace is wide enough to reach every soul and personal enough to redeem mine.

Prayer

Savior of the World, thank You for coming to rescue what was lost. Your love knows no boundaries. Forgive me when I forget that Your grace extends to everyone, even those I find hardest to love. Use my life to reflect Your mercy and share Your good news wherever I go. Let my heart overflow with gratitude for the salvation You freely give. Amen.

Journaling Prompt

- What does it mean to you that Jesus came for the whole world — including you personally?
- How might you share the hope of His salvation with someone this Christmas season?
- Write a prayer thanking Jesus for including you in His story of redemption.

Verse to Write

"For the Son of Man came to seek and to save the lost."
— *Luke 19:10 (NIV)*

Reflection Break

As we inch near Christmas Day, pause to pray for the people who are open to receive them. Ask God to use even the simplest acts of kindness to point others to the Savior of the World — the greatest gift ever given.

December 21

The King of Kings

Scripture Focus

> *"On his robe and on his thigh he has this name written:*
> *KING OF KINGS AND LORD OF LORDS."*
> *— Revelation 19:16 (NIV)*

Reflection

E very kingdom on earth eventually fades. History books are filled with the rise and fall of empires, the names of rulers who once held power and then passed away. But there is one King whose reign will never end. His name is Jesus — the King of Kings and Lord of Lords.

From the moment of His birth, His kingship was both proclaimed and misunderstood. Wise men came from the east asking, "Where is the one who has been born king of the Jews?" They offered Him royal gifts of gold, frankincense, and myrrh.

Yet His throne was a feeding trough, His attendants shepherds, and His first decree the soft cry of an infant.

Throughout His ministry, Jesus spoke often of His kingdom. It was not built on conquest but compassion, not advanced by armies but by love. When Pilate asked if He was a king, Jesus replied, "My kingdom is not of this world." He wore no crown of gold, only a crown of thorns. And yet, in that moment of apparent defeat, He accomplished His greatest victory. The cross that looked like surrender became His coronation. The tomb that seemed like loss became the doorway to His eternal throne. The Lamb who was slain now reigns as the Lion who conquers.

Advent reminds us that the baby in the manger was born to rule, not by force but by faithful love. His kingdom begins in human hearts and extends across every nation. He rules with justice and mercy, offering peace to those who surrender to His reign. One day, the waiting will end. The King of Kings will return, not in humility but in glory. Every knee will bow and every tongue will confess that He is Lord. The heavens will resound with worship, and His kingdom will have no end.

Until that day, we live as citizens of His kingdom, reflecting His values in how we love and serve. Each time we choose forgiveness over bitterness, truth over comfort, or faith over fear, we declare that Jesus is our King. As you prepare for Christmas, perhaps while setting your table or finishing last-minute shopping, take a moment to picture that final celebration — the true royal banquet where every tribe and tongue will praise the King. The sparkle of holiday lights is only a shadow of His glory. This is the promise of Advent: the King has come, the King still reigns, and the King will return.

Daily Affirmation

Jesus is the King of Kings. His reign is eternal, His rule is righteous, and His love governs my heart.

Prayer

King of Kings, I worship You as the ruler of all creation. Thank You for leading with justice, mercy, and love. Help me live as a loyal citizen of Your kingdom, reflecting Your goodness to others. May my heart bow before You daily, and my life proclaim Your glory until You return. Amen.

Journaling Prompt

- What does it mean to live as a citizen of Christ's kingdom in today's world?
- How can you honor Jesus as King in your decisions, your home, and your relationships?
- Write a short prayer of worship, declaring His kingship over your life.

Verse to Write

"The Lord will be king over the whole earth.
  On that day there will be one Lord, and his name the only name."
  — Zechariah 14:9 (NIV)

Reflection Break

Pause to worship the One who reigns above all as you listen to Christmas carols or see a nativity scene today. Whisper a prayer of adoration: "Jesus, You are my King." Let that truth crown your heart with peace today.

December 22

The Alpha and Omega

Scripture Focus

"I am the Alpha and the Omega," says the Lord God,
"who is, and who was, and who is to come, the
Almighty."
— *Revelation 1:8 (NIV)*

Reflection

E very story begins somewhere, but only one begins and ends with the same Person. In Revelation, Jesus declares Himself the Alpha and the Omega—the first and last letters of the Greek alphabet. The phrase means more than "beginning and end." It means He is the source of all things and the One who brings everything to completion. Nothing starts without Him, and nothing will finish apart from Him.

When John received his vision on the island of Patmos, the

church was facing fierce persecution. It would have been easy to wonder if the story of faith was coming to an end. But through that revelation, Christ reminded His people that history is not spiraling out of control. Every moment, from creation to eternity, rests securely in His hands.

Jesus was there in the beginning, speaking galaxies into being. He was present in Bethlehem, wrapped in humanity. He will be there at the end, reigning in glory. The same Lord who formed the world will one day renew it. His sovereignty spans all time, yet His love reaches each moment personally.

When life feels uncertain, this name becomes an anchor. The Alpha reminds us that God started our story with purpose. The Omega assures us that He will finish what He began. We may not understand every chapter, but He does. Every joy, sorrow, and detour fits within His perfect plan. Advent draws our hearts toward beginnings—the beginning of hope, light, and salvation. But it also reminds us that this story isn't over. The manger was not the conclusion; it was the continuation of a plan written before time began. The child born in Bethlehem is the same Lord who will one day bring creation to its final redemption.

Today, think about the beauty of beginnings and endings. The glow of the lights, the hush of a winter evening, the anticipation of celebration—all of it points to a God who authors every moment with intention. You can trust Him with the past He has already redeemed, the present He sustains, and the future He holds. From Alpha to Omega, His faithfulness never wavers.

Daily Affirmation

Jesus is the Alpha and the Omega. He began my story, sustains my present, and will complete His good work in me.

Prayer

Eternal Lord, thank You for holding every moment of my life in Your hands. When I am tempted to fear what's ahead, remind me that You are already there. You are my beginning and my end, my origin and my destiny. Teach me to rest in Your sovereignty and to trust the story You are still writing. Amen.

Journaling Prompt

- Which part of your life feels unfinished or uncertain right now?
- How does knowing that Jesus is both the beginning and the end bring you peace?
- Write a prayer of surrender, entrusting every chapter of your story to Him.

Verse to Write

> *"Jesus Christ is the same yesterday and today and for-ever."*
> — *Hebrews 13:8 (NIV)*

Reflection Break

Take a quiet evening moment to reflect on this year—its highs, lows, and in-betweens. Thank Jesus for being present in every season. Whisper these words as a prayer of confidence: "You are my Alpha and my Omega."

December 23

The True Light

Scripture Focus

"The true light that gives light to everyone was coming into the world."
   — *John 1:9 (NIV)*

Reflection

From the very beginning, light has marked God's work. "Let there be light," He spoke, and darkness fled. From that moment, light became a symbol of His presence, purity, and power. In the Old Testament, God led His people with a pillar of fire by night. His glory filled the temple with radiant brilliance. Yet all those glimmers were reflections of something greater—the coming of the True Light.

When John wrote his Gospel, he introduced Jesus with cosmic language. The eternal Word who was with God and was God became flesh and entered a darkened world as the True Light. His arrival didn't simply illuminate a stable in Bethlehem; it pierced the spiritual darkness that sin had cast over creation.

Light exposes what is hidden, reveals what is real, and makes the way clear. Jesus does all of that and more. His light exposes sin not to shame us but to free us. It reveals truth in a world clouded by confusion. It shows the way to the Father through faith. Everywhere Jesus went, darkness retreated. Demons fled. Despair lifted. Eyes once blind began to see. The same power that shone in first-century Galilee still shines in our hearts today. As John later wrote, "The darkness has not overcome it."

During the Christmas season, we're surrounded by light. Strings of bulbs outline rooftops. Candles flicker in windows. Fireplaces glow with warmth. All of these lights are small echoes of the True Light—the One who came not to decorate the world, but to deliver it. Yet even now, it's easy to feel the weight of darkness. Grief, fear, or the brokenness of our world can make the night seem long. Advent doesn't deny that darkness exists; it proclaims that it doesn't win. The Light has come, and the shadows cannot stand against it.

Today, every time you see a light, pause to remember that every flicker, from the magnificent sun to the tiniest bulb, points to a far greater truth: the Light of the World lives within you. His light isn't fragile; it's unstoppable. You don't have to create it—just reflect it.

Daily Affirmation

Jesus is the True Light. His truth guides me, His grace warms me, and His presence shines through me.

Prayer

True Light of Heaven, thank You for breaking through the darkness with Your glory. When my world feels dim, remind me that Your light still burns strong. Shine through me in kindness, words, and actions so that others may see You. Fill my home and heart with the radiance of Your presence this Christmas. Amen.

Journaling Prompt

- Where do you see glimpses of God's light in your life right now?
- What areas of your heart need His light to bring healing or direction?
- Write about how you can reflect His light to someone who feels stuck in darkness.

Verse to Write

"You, Lord, keep my lamp burning; my God turns my darkness into light."
   — *Psalm 18:28 (NIV)*

Reflection Break

Take a deep breath and thank Jesus for being your True Light. Pray that His love will shine through you today—bright enough to warm the hearts around you.

December 24

The Name Above All Names

Scripture Focus

"Therefore God exalted him to the highest place
and gave him the name that is above every name,
that at the name of Jesus every knee should bow,
in heaven and on earth and under the earth,
and every tongue acknowledge that Jesus Christ is Lord,
to the glory of God the Father."
— Philippians 2:9–11 (NIV)

Reflection

There are names that carry history, titles that bring honor, and then there is **Jesus** — the name above all names. The name spoken by angels before His birth, whispered by shepherds in wonder, and worshiped by kings who traveled far to find Him. It is the name that has outlasted empires, calmed storms, and still brings peace to hearts in turmoil.

The apostle Paul wrote these words to the Philippians to remind them that greatness in God's kingdom looks like humility. Jesus, though fully God, chose to humble Himself — born not in a palace but in a stable, laid not in a cradle of gold but in a manger of straw. He emptied Himself of status to lift us from sin. Because of that obedience, God exalted Him to the highest place and gave Him the highest name.

On this quiet Christmas Eve night, we remember that His exaltation began in His humiliation. The path to glory ran through Bethlehem, Nazareth, Calvary, and an empty tomb. The name of Jesus holds power because it carries the weight of redemption. It is the name that demons fear and believers cherish, the name through which we are saved and by which prayers reach heaven. When you speak His name, you are not uttering mere syllables. You are calling on the very presence of God. The name *Jesus* means "The Lord saves." Every time we say it, we declare the heart of the gospel.

Tonight, as the world slows and anticipation fills the air, consider the beauty of that name. It has crossed centuries and cultures, healing hearts, restoring hope, and transforming lives. No other name carries such tenderness or such authority.

Advent has been a season of waiting, reflection, and hope. But this night — Christmas Eve — turns waiting into worship. It invites us to kneel beside shepherds and wise men, to lift our voices with angels, and to whisper the name that changed everything: Jesus. When you wrap the last gift or sit in the glow of your tree tonight, let your heart rest in that name. Whatever tomorrow holds, the One who bears that precious name is faithful. His name will never fade, and His reign will never end.

Daily Affirmation

Jesus is the Name above all names. I bow my heart to His authority and lift my voice in praise to His glory.

Prayer

Jesus, there is no other name like Yours. Your name brings peace where there is fear, hope where there is sorrow, and light where there is darkness. On this Christmas Eve, I worship You as Savior, Lord, and King. May Your name be exalted around the world as it is in my heart and in my home tonight and always. Amen.

Journaling Prompt

- What does the name "Jesus" mean to you personally?
- How have you experienced His power or peace this Advent season?
- Write a prayer of worship, thanking Him for all that His name represents.

Verse to Write

"Salvation is found in no one else, for there is no other name under heaven given to mankind by which we must be saved."

— Acts 4:12 (NIV)

Reflection Break

Before you go to bed tonight, sit quietly in the soft light of your Christmas decorations. Whisper His name — *Jesus.* Let that single word fill the room and your heart. The wait is over. The Light of the world has come.

December 25

Jesus, Messiah

Scripture Focus

> *"Today in the town of David a Savior has been born to you;*
>> *he is the Messiah, the Lord."*
>> *— Luke 2:11 (NIV)*

Reflection

The wait is over. The silence has broken. The promise has arrived. After centuries of prophecy and generations of longing, the Messiah—the Anointed One—has come.

That word, *Messiah* (or *Christos* in Greek), means "the Anointed One." In ancient Israel, kings, prophets, and priests were anointed with oil to set them apart for God's purpose. But Jesus was not just another anointed servant. He was the fulfillment of them all—the King who reigns forever, the Prophet who reveals the Father, and the High Priest who reconciles us to God.

The night of His birth was quiet, yet heaven could not stay silent. Angels filled the sky with glory, declaring, "A Savior has been born to you; he is the Messiah, the Lord." The announcement was not given to emperors or priests but to shepherds—ordinary men watching over their flocks. The first to hear the good news were those who understood what it meant to care for lambs.

The One born that night would one day be called the Lamb of God, offering His life to redeem the world. But for this moment, in the stillness of Bethlehem, the Messiah lay wrapped in cloth, resting in a manger—a King with no crown but infinite authority. Christmas morning is the convergence of heaven and earth. The Word became flesh. The Creator stepped into creation. Every promise God had ever made found its "yes" in Jesus.

When we call Him "Messiah," we acknowledge that He is not only the long-awaited Redeemer of Israel but the Savior of all humanity. He came to heal what was broken, restore what was lost, and bring peace between God and His people. As you wake this morning, perhaps to laughter, the smell of cinnamon rolls, or the rustle of wrapping paper, pause for a holy moment. This is the day that changed every other day. The true gift of Christmas isn't found beneath a tree but in a manger—God's presence dwelling with us.

The Messiah has come for you. Not because you earned it, but because love Himself could not stay away. His birth was the beginning of your redemption story, one that stretches from

Bethlehem to Calvary to eternity. Today, let joy fill your heart. The waiting has given way to wonder. The promise has become a Person. His name is Jesus, Messiah.

Daily Affirmation

Jesus is my Messiah. He fulfills every promise, redeems every story, and reigns forever as my Savior and King.

Prayer

Messiah, my Lord, my Redeemer—thank You for coming to save. On this Christmas morning, fill my heart with gratitude for the miracle of Your birth. Let the joy of Your presence be my song, and may my life declare that You are the promised One, the hope of the world. Amen.

Journaling Prompt

- What part of Jesus' story has touched your heart most deeply this Advent season?
- How can you carry the hope of Christmas into the year ahead?
- Write a prayer of praise, thanking Jesus for being your Messiah and the fulfillment of every promise.

Verse to Write

"For no matter how many promises God has made, they are 'Yes' in Christ.
And so through him the 'Amen' is spoken by us to the

glory of God."
 — *2 Corinthians 1:20 (NIV)*

Reflection Break

Take a few minutes this Christmas day to step away from the noise and simply worship. Whisper a quiet "thank You" to the Messiah who came for you. Let your heart rest in the miracle of Emmanuel—God with us, now and forever.

Bonus: 25 Breath Prayers

What is a Scripture-based breath prayer?

A Scripture-based breath prayer is a short line of Scripture (or truth drawn directly from it) prayed in rhythm with your breathing. It helps you quiet your mind, focus your heart on God, and keep His Word close throughout the day.

How it works:

1. **Choose a verse** or phrase from Scripture.
2. **Inhale** as you pray the first half.
3. **Exhale** as you pray the second half.
4. Repeat for 1–3 minutes whenever you need calm or focus.

Why it helps:

- Anchors attention in God's Word, not feelings.
- Calms the body while nurturing the soul.
- Easy to remember and pray anywhere.

Example (Psalm 23:1):

- **Inhale:** "The Lord is my shepherd..."
- **Exhale:** "...I shall not want."

Please enjoy these 25 bonus breath prayers as a companion for He Shall Be Called: A 25-Day Advent Devotional for Praying the Names of Jesus:

1. Wonderful Counselor- Isaiah 9:6
   Inhale: Wonderful Counselor, give me Your wisdom.
   Exhale: Teach me the way I should go.

2. Mighty God- Isaiah 9:6
   Inhale: Mighty God, be my strength today.
   Exhale: I trust Your power, not my own.

3. Everlasting Father- Isaiah 9:6
   Inhale: Everlasting Father, draw me close.
   Exhale: I rest in Your unending love.

4. Prince of Peace- Isaiah 9:6
   Inhale: Prince of Peace, settle my spirit.
   Exhale: Let Your peace rule my heart.

5. Emmanuel- Matthew 1:23
   Inhale: Emmanuel—God with us.
   Exhale: Be with me here and now.

6. The Word- John 1:1

Inhale: In the beginning was the Word.
Exhale: Speak Your life into me.

7. The Lamb of God- John 1:29
Inhale: Lamb of God, I behold You.
Exhale: Take away my sin; make me new.

8. The Good Shepherd- John 10:11
Inhale: Good Shepherd, lead me today.
Exhale: I follow Your voice and rest in Your care.

9. The Light of the World- John 8:12
Inhale: Light of the world, guide my steps.
Exhale: I will not walk in darkness.

10. The Bread of Life- John 6:35
Inhale: Bread of Life, nourish my soul.
Exhale: In You I will not hunger or thirst.

11. The Way, the Truth, and the Life- John 14:6
Inhale: Jesus, You are the Way, the Truth, the Life.
Exhale: I follow You to the Father.

12. The True Vine- John 15:1-2
Inhale: True Vine, prune what hinders
Exhale: That I may bear fruit.

13. The Son of Man- Mark 10:45
Inhale: Son of Man, You came to serve.
Exhale: Make me a servant in your likeness.

14. The Great High Priest- Hebrews 4:14-15
Inhale: Great High Priest, You know my weakness.
Exhale: Keep me near—help me hold fast.

15. The Healer- Isaiah 53:5
Inhale: Pierced for my transgressions—
Exhale: By Your wounds, heal me wholly.

16. The Bridegroom- John 3:29
Inhale: Bridegroom, I wait and listen.
Exhale: Let Your voice be my joy.

17. The Cornerstone- Ephesians 2:19-20
Inhale: Christ my Cornerstone,
Exhale: Build me on Your sure foundation.

18. The Lion of Judah- Revelation 5:5
Inhale: Lion of Judah, give me courage.
Exhale: You have triumphed—my hope is secure.

19. The Resurrection and the Life- John 11:25-26
Inhale: Jesus, Resurrection and Life,
Exhale: I believe Your life conquers my death.

20. The Savior of the World- John 4:42
Inhale: Savior of the World,
Exhale: my rescue and hope.

21. The King of Kings- Revelation 19:16
Inhale: King of Kings, reign in me.
Exhale: Lord of Lords, Your rule endures forever.

22. The Alpha and the Omega- Revelation 1:8
   Inhale: Alpha and Omega, hold my days.
   Exhale: You were, You are, You are to come.

23. The True Light- John 1:9
   Inhale: True Light, illumine my heart.
   Exhale: Shine in me and scatter every shadow.

24. The Name Above All Names- Philippians 2:9-11
   Inhale: Jesus, Name above every name.
   Exhale: I bow to You—You are Lord.

25. Jesus, Messiah- Luke 2:11
   Inhale: Today a Savior is born to us.
   Exhale: Jesus, Messiah, my Lord.

Conclusion

Closing Reflection — Carrying the Light Beyond Christmas

T he candles have burned low. The wrapping paper is gone. The carols fade to silence. And yet the story continues. For the past four weeks, Christians have been preparing to celebrate Jesus' birth in Bethlehem. At the same time, Advent also looks **ahead** to His promised and glorious return in the future. We remember His first coming and ready our hearts for His second. So Christmas Eve doesn't end Advent's message; it reveals its heart. It celebrates the Incarnation—God becoming human in Jesus and living among us—and reminds us that the same Jesus who once came near now meets us in our everyday lives, turning ordinary moments into sacred ground.

The manger led to a cross. The cross led to an empty tomb. And the empty tomb leads to you — to your heart, your home, your life. The King who came still comes. The Light that dawned in Bethlehem still shines in bedrooms and kitchens, classrooms and hospital rooms. You may pack away ornaments, but never pack away wonder. Let the names of Jesus you've learned over these twenty-five days become living truths you carry into January and beyond.

When you need wisdom, call on the Wonderful Counselor. When fear knocks, remember the Mighty God. When anxiety whispers, rest in the Prince of Peace. When life feels dim, look to the True Light. When you doubt your worth, remember the Lamb who chose you. This is the rhythm of the redeemed — to live Advent every day.

So as the year turns and the noise returns, pause often. Breathe His name. Let "Emmanuel, God with us," become your anthem in the quiet moments and the crowded ones alike because the story that began in Bethlehem has no end. The Child in the manger is the King on the throne. And the One who came for the world has not stopped coming for you.

Author's Note

When I first began writing *He Shall Be Called: A 25-Day Advent Devotional for Praying the Names of Jesus,* I didn't realize it would become a journey that healed parts of me I didn't even know were broken. Each name of Jesus reminded me that faith isn't about understanding every detail — it's about trusting the One who holds them all together. If you've made it to these final pages, my hope is that this devotional has done more than fill your mornings or evenings. I pray it has brought you closer to the One whose love never fails, whose promises never expire, and whose presence never leaves.

The story of Jesus didn't end in Bethlehem, and your story doesn't end here either. Keep seeking Him in every season — in laughter and loss, in worship and waiting. Let His names anchor you when life feels uncertain and lift you when hope flickers low. Thank you for letting me walk beside you through this Advent journey. It's a sacred thing to share words about a Savior who changes everything.

May His peace go with you, and may His many names stay on your lips long after the lights of Christmas fade.

With love and gratitude,
   Tracey Grumbach

About the Author

Tracey Grumbach is an author, publisher, educator, and creative entrepreneur who believes that every story, every song, and every sunrise points back to the Creator. After three decades as a teacher, she founded **Grumpy Dog Publishing, LLC,** and its faith division, **Veritas Spring**, to help others encounter God through Scripture, art, and worship music.

Tracey writes from her small farm in White Hall, Maryland, where she and her husband, Brian, share life with their horse, cat, and two high-spirited Brussels Griffon dogs. Their four exceptional adult children remain her greatest earthly joy and constant inspiration.

Through devotionals like *He Shall Be Called: A 25-Day Advent*

Devotional for Praying the Names of Jesus, she invites believers to slow down, breathe deep, and rediscover the beauty of walking with Jesus day by day.

You can connect with me on:

🌐 https://www.veritasspring.com

📘 https://www.facebook.com/veritasspring

www.ingramcontent.com/pod-product-compliance
Lightning Source LLC
Chambersburg PA
CBHW060811050426
42449CB00008B/1633